Arguing with Malarchy

CAROLA LUTHER was born in South Africa and moved to Britain in 1981. She lives and works in Yorkshire. Her first book, *Walking the Animals*, published by Carcanet, was shortlisted for the Forward Prize for best first collection in 2004.

Also by Carola Luther

Walking the Animals

CAROLA LUTHER

Arguing with Malarchy

CARCANET

First published in Great Britain in 2011 by
Carcanet Press Limited
Alliance House
Cross Street
Manchester M2 7AQ

A CIP catalogue record for this book is available from the British Library

ISBN 978 1 84777 093 6

The publisher acknowledges financial assistance from Arts Council England

Typeset by XL Publishing Services, Tiverton
Printed and bound in England by SRP Ltd, Exeter

for Sheila

Acknowledgements

Acknowledgements are due to the editors of: *NW 14: The Anthology of New Writing, Volume 14* (Granta Books and the British Council, 2006), *Parameter, PN Review, Poetry London, The Bridport Prize Anthology 2004* (Sansom and Company), *Signs and Humours: The Poetry of Medicine* (Calouste Gulbenkian Foundation, 2007) and to the *Guardian* feature 'Exit Wounds', 25 July 2009. Thank you.

Thanks also to the Nes Artists Residency in Iceland, and the people of Skagaströnd for their kindness and hospitality, and the opportunity to spend a month on their beautiful peninsula.

Acknowledgements and thanks to Jenni Molloy, composer and musician, who collaborated with me in adapting the Malarchy sequence into a performance piece. Also to Sheila Tilmouth, artist and photographer, for the cover photo.

Thanks to Lynn Alderson, Zetta Bear, Ruth Bowen, Stephanie Bowgett, John Duffy, Mair Felix, Sheila Kershaw, Anne Landsman, Olwen May, Chris Preddle and all the members of the Albert Poetry Workshop for their encouragement, careful reading, and invaluable feedback.

To Lyn Romeo and Linda Anderson for lending me their peaceful homes to write in.

To the editors of Carcanet, Michael Schmidt and Judith Willson, my thanks and appreciation.

Lastly, I am grateful to the poet Linda Chase. I remember with thanks her generosity, comradeship and open-hearted encouragement.

Contents

Part I: *Cusp*

Part II: *Acres*

I

Cusp

I watch the bees slow down the summer

I watch the bees slow down the summer. Honeysuckle sink
beneath their substance. Sunlit busbies stuffed with sleep
and ochre powder making journeys, wavery, vague,
full of just-remembered purpose, so I come to think
of aged gardeners, with their pots and hats and secret
pockets full of dust, casting stuff on yellow air so seconds
stretch (a whole long summer each, if we could only enter them)
a gift of sorts, for us, a hunch, as if they've guessed, the bees,
and understood the rock at the garden's end, the crouching
sky, the path on its narrow belly, dropping to the sea.

get out of town, driving your car fast along the new ring road,
going west for a mile and swerving hard left at the junction,
following the diversion for a few hundred yards to the crossroads,
turning right, and right again over the bridge, before the sharp
left corner which you take swiftly, changing down a gear
as you twist between pylons to make the short cut
through the disused warehouse, heading in the direction
of the road to the sea, and here you'll pick up
the first lane you come to, which appears to turn inland
but doubles back in fact upon itself, bringing you out
several miles on between a quarry and a V-shaped spinney
of trees, and just a little further, in unkempt countryside
you can slow right down, looking for where a shadow of a track
meets the lane at a mound, and bear left here, and keep bearing
left, continuing through woods to a clump of the darkest
and most silent pines, and when it feels possible, and in the distance
you begin to think it probable that the moors will open out
on every side, bring the vehicle to a stop, anywhere
where a pool of sunlight may be found. Turn off the engine
and look at your hands. Look at the sun on your knuckles,
the folds and grooves of skin over the joints
of your fingers, the way the veins rise above the fine
hand-bones like tributaries of a dark grey river,
how two grey branches almost meet between the third finger
and the fourth, how the shadows plummet here
into the ravine between them, how going over the edge
in a small canoe would contact rock-white water
drumming through the rapids in the rolling dark
plunging in and out of the roar of the river and turning
over, and over, and over, and calming right down
in the slow shallow width of the palm,
and beginning to drift between reeds of the delta,
you'll manoeuvre later through tricky marsh islands,
and somewhere here disembark and meander
through dunes to the deep-cut valley of the heart,
and falling in a basket made of rushes
you'll bask in the sun, feeling the thrum

of the water beneath you bearing you onward
to the place where the fate line crosses, and allowing
the hollowed-out log that you now lie down in,
clothed in the swathes of your white linen clothes,
you'll follow the inexorable pull of the current
towards the slopes of the mountain of Venus,
and from the summit if you decide to climb it,
you will see the road carved at the wrist
glimmering and pale beside ancestral bracelets,
and life keeping time like the heartbeat of bird
held in, held together, by a few twig bones,
the thinnest of skins.

Julia's Party

Little more than ligament
she swayed
over her knuckles,
held up by her stick,
in her drooping fields of cloth.

Maxim Maxim Maxim
she looked as if she might call
(like anyone would hear her now!)

What was she thinking, down here
amongst the young,
firm as new salad
in their heedless limbs,
careless of their bodies
as they lean towards bodies
draped over the balcony
films of themselves
playing
in each others eyes?

(Behind us, the night spread
towards France. The bay was a gentle neck
looped with beads
the sea, a brother
asleep at home, breathing softly
in a yellow room.)

Something to announce:
she lifted her stick with both her hands,
waved it eastward and westward
like a sherpa's flag, or a frond
for Cleopatra in an old school play
or as if she wanted to say
fill up your glasses, turtles
this one's on me, dum, diddy
dum, oh listen to that horn,

that conga drum, this,
little chameleons
this is my song

On the other hand of course
we might have got it wrong
and this was code for *help*
you stupid buggers –
signal, morse –
flood-
throat-
heart-
burst-

But she didn't get them out
the words, before folding up
like a deckchair, kicked
right there against the yellow doors,
their spilled yellow mist.

Afterwards someone wondered
what we might have heard
(had one of us, through the evening
offered her our arm)
imagining perhaps
an axiom on her lips,
something stunned and simple,
like the answer to a puzzle
that had been understood at last
and lost.

After the Funeral

Sky blue despite predictions
of snow.

Sky blue for two days
despite predictions of snow.

Sky blue through your picture
window despite predictions of wind

and snow. (The wind a keening leash
day and night, polecats, weasels, stoats

regretful, keening, gutter narrow.)
Sky blue through your balcony window-frame

despite the narrow wind. Sky blue
filling your huge balcony window-frame

with tales of travel despite the lament
of the narrow-backed wind.

Sky blue and planes traversing
the glassy screen of your window.

Five planes and two birds travailing across
the clear glass blue

of your balcony window.
Sky blue and two gulls.

Three planes
and two vapour trails.

Two short white trails splitting
the blue glass window.

Sky blue framed. Two planes
no trails, no birds, wind.

Sky blue framed, one plane
no birds. Sky blue, no birds

no planes, the narrow wind.
Sky blue your window.

It's not allowed
but if I could
I would float naked
when I am dead
just beneath the water
of the tawny river
facing the yellow sky.

Pass through the tree's
reflection balanced on
its substance, see
the dangling branches
in ripples of the sky.
Catch a pale self, staring
down at me, the floating

circle of a shivered
bridge. Watch her
think she's seen me
drifting up and under
like something half-
remembered, half-known
half-loved, half-lived.

Cusp

That morning, it was more than frost. I saw
we stood on the cusp, the trees and I. Imagined
they imagined, in the thin line of rime

both the soot and blossom of themselves.
The shape of each tree was stark, their darkness
outlined by a line of white, possibility

powdery, bright, and dropping in clumps
at the smallest out-breath of breeze, floating
diagonally like blossom after the bees have done,

as if it was warm – or otherwise old-fashioned
cold and these powders were flowers of snow.
It was all X-ray, tomograph, scan. As if to move

towards death or give birth was the choice
to be made in the moments before mist
was burnt off by the sun. I could see the heart

of each tree, crystal, etched. Each tree in the park
itself entirely, twice itself, in black, and in white.
The hanging willow, the hands-up spruce

the bandaged ends of the sycamore twigs
the straight-up beech. And those two woodpigeons,
still and hunched, balanced like ash-covered fruits

on the silk-white branch of the birch. A breeze
picking up. They would have been doves
if they could. They would have been doves.

Hold on to the sky

for K

Hold on to the sky –
it is unchanging
and changing,
cradle and longing
of reliable trees.
It bears the passing
cargo of cloud,
or shows the ocean
its own blue face
so it knows what it is
and how it is named.
It is where birds discover
their intricate runes,
and moths lose the last
of their blind white leaves.
From there, Venus
drops rings into night-eyes
of creatures, the moon's
habit of loss moves
beaches of stone.
Hold on to the sky
all through the darkness,
hold on, hold on –
a small blue rag
of the sky.

Vernal

I watch the clouds graze,
how gently they move
keeping their backs to the soft cold
breeze. I am on my back
spreading my arms
in their own warm circle.

If I was six feet under, or even one,
today is the day when I would work
knuckles through the soil
push my last bundle
upward to the sun
and unfold bone-white
bells to shiver, to ring
across the long blue field of the sky.

Easter

Something stirring under the mud, the nosing of buds
the nudging of tubers, and a sudden frog with planetary
rings in its eyes giving birth by my head, purring, purring
pouring out eggs, jellied dots and jellied specks, a lidless
pile of eyes keeping watch round three hundred and sixty
degrees of night and day, while under here the tiresome
boiling of spring, the growths, the growing around me
shifting the crook of my root once again, so I cannot rest
cannot resist the living horde pulling against the grain
of my limb, I turn my hip, I will not look, but still I feel
the skyward suck and a warm dim green on my bones.
Let go Let go I hear the birds, the frogs, the dogs that bark
the fox that sits and stares me out through the holes
in the trembling reflection of its orange and ochre eyes.
I sigh. I'm lost and found. A green blood pounds
through the stem that's breaking the skin of the pond,
and despite depletion I find I want to smile at the tickle
of tadpoles caught in the leaves, and with a jolt
I remember the feel of wanting *to greet*, to touch across distance;
and come to understand that I am *waving*; that the vivid
kingcup unfolding its yellow for the palm of the sun,
is, petal by petal, the bole of my opening hand.

The Lamb

It saw me walking over the hill,
came to its knees and ran. I placed
my hands on the flattened grass
where that newborn lamb had lain.
The pressed down grass was warm,
a curved green print of lamb,
and I found I wanted to lay me down
in the place where that lamb had been.
I found I wanted to lay me down
and wait for my friend, the lion.

he did sing
            the bare threads of tunes
and weave them perhaps
into something
        like gaily-plaited gentlies
held
        to hold
softly in his hand
            similar to birds or reins   time   or thereabouts
for a short while dozed
        doze   slow

in his hand these songs
gaily-plaiteds on an old horse
gallant   known
finding its own way through the leaves
when perhaps we sat outside
on lichen-splattered wood in sun
            or nearly
regarding trees and bees and
                        scars of tiny planes
expanding infinitesimally in the sky

a bird-shaped scar
high-hearted on his hand
singing as it reached its loop
            tip
and hung there slow   slowed
        slow all things
the frantic wings of dragonflies mid-beat above the yellow iris
and the bees
        dozed
and the birds
        dozed
and the old dog and the old horse

                 dozed
though hooves kept dropping softly in that song
                              turf
                              leaf
                  hooves softly falling
                              hooves
                    hooves

Smiling for the Camera

I spend all day watching the sea as if something
is going to come out of it, dragging sleevefuls
of seaweed and opening its maw to sing.
Something needs to throw back its head and sing
for love or liberty, or perhaps more truly, the country
you were for me – look – a person could eat
with those quick little sticks the sanderling wobbles on,
running to keep itself clear of the waves. And the house,
propped up in sunlight with holiday bravado, as if
its bright washing were a canopy in Spain. We have this
thing, all of us, smiling for the camera. I watch
all afternoon. Colour spreads evening right across
the water, staining the seabirds crouched in their bowls.
They tuck in their heads and legs. They rock.
Who knows if they have been cheerful all day, really?
Who would know now, if they were sad or cold?

Making Peace

For it might have been a rhythm
like the tying of knots
as if we had been mending nets for the fish together
or making nets, or sacks for oranges
long ago in a hot country.

The hitch, the slip, the loop
of nothing much into separate pockets,
the smell of sea drying on rocks
in the setting sun; or in the morning sun
the singing that could have been crying
on the red road
and the smell of hot, heaped fruit.

The way the talk came and broke
streaming backward and forward
and leaving behind the outline
of something that reminded us of itself,
a debris of salt and empty shells and bags
and rubbery ribbons of fields
of the sea. Perhaps the body of a weird fish, half lost
to itself, bringing to mind the impossible
cycads crouched to the north. The weight
of silence when it came, which it would
wherever we might be, black and clenched
as midday shade, umbrella upturned
beneath an orange tree.
And the polished flies reclaiming the pile,
the stench of solids melting to syrup
under the stir of their blue metal spoons, the heat
of the white metal sun.
And everywhere the scream of cicadas
clubbing it all the way to the future
pumping their legs in their techno rhythms,
stoned and alone in their midday millions,
presaging from somewhere, sometime
a lethal and answering rage.

And all the while the old-fashioned business
of ordinary fury and the stubbornness of love
could be said to be moving
through our conversations,
as if these were our labouring fingers
drawing imaginary thread through the unnamed
and invisible fabrics of the sky,
knotting tight or intricate knots
around sudden squares of laughter,
our resting hands. Framed
and full of faces, the shapes in sand
or orange-skins, phosphorescent traces
of migrations, the slow ways found by rivers.
An album of sorts,
this making or mending of nets,
rough squares, bulging
with the myriad pictures of air.

Dreaming the Dead

How hard to find your shape the further you move
and by now so used to the running dunes of light. A form

of resentment perhaps, at the tugging insistence, the cry
that echoes through caves and conduits awaking the infant

at the very beginning, gone but remembered, the need
to remember outlining old matters, pulling a familiar finger

or foot from what is invisible, the menstruum of possible
or imagined or is. Not you as you were, but some aspect or snap

of a repetitive heart, requiring your neck or your arm or your eyes
(so often your eyes, most demanding of all) the duct

to the darkness of light, the light of the dark you knew at the time,
not now, not now, not soon. How heavy the memory of flesh

worn in the course of this duty, becoming this person
you hardly know any more, how much more arduous

than substance of dik-dik or duiker, the sweeping wet weight
of blue whale. How you must long to be called instead

to manifest light in the ululant slip of a quick desert snake,
the vibration of bee, the green monkey-parabola,

kaleidoscopes of tunes in sun-running waters,
the sound from the mouth of a different, a laughing child.

Letters from the Peninsula

Skagaströnd, November 2008

What is found
and lost: dried up kelp
like letters burnt.

Lumps in the tundra
that could be the half-buried
heads of the dead, as if all the boys and girls
sent to war are here, half-risen
on this lawn of warriors, half-risen,
half-sung, half-finished.
What are they thinking, these children
with their powerful skulls and half-shaved heads?
What are the words they mouthe?

The Stone Age horses.
Their long wheat hair.

The sadness of the horse and its foal
snuffling for something on a blackened beach,
a tiny food of taste or sustenance,
while in the distance the town
waits, watching for something from sea or sky,
every window following the light.

Tonight, stars crack the dark.

The low house
like my own pet animal
keeps out snow with sounds,
its comforting habits.

New tones of darkness, shades
of pallor, degrees of milky white.

A flotilla of gulls:
swimmers in their caps
congregating before the winter race.

Mountains
quietly arming.

The half dark of day,
grass surpassing itself,
each blade becoming
a custodian of light.

Mountains striped like arctic cats
camouflaged as sky.
When our backs are turned
they'll creep closer
on bellies and stony elbows.

Quiet herds of mountains
overlooking the horses.

The people, some with pale eyes
for garnering the light,
others darker
for burning the snow.

Mountains
not penned in.

Fishermen rubbed
and silenced.
All that closeness
to the iris of the sea.

Fish piled high
like the dead of a conquered planet.
No exceptions: vast old warriors,
nuns, senators, queens
even the jailors
with their clean metal keys.

In their greys
the poor fade fast.
Robes of bishops and dancers of the court
take longer.

The sorrow,
the half-closed lips of fishes.

Eyes wide open,
their stretched, wrenched
mouths.

Red.
Blue.
Turquoise.
Yellow.
Bright houses.
Square flowers
of the snow.

The bus driver's radio,
louder and louder
the further away
from the city we get,
as if he's afraid
the signal will soon go down,
that he might forget
the arms of his woman,
his cube of kitchen,
bread, soup, light
his only son
fringed like a changeling
or a dark-maned horse
and playing soft songs
on his father's guitar.

On the beach
the end of so many things:
kelp like a wrestler's belt
when the competition's lost,
tyres, a ball, an untoothed shoe.
And who would have expected
the rubberiness of starfish,
something broken nonetheless,
fingertips bent backward
like mutilated gloves.

All that seaweed:
arms wrenched from sockets,
heaps hardly moving
too recently torn
from their roots.

Anemone-shells the colour of crowberries
mussels the colour of crowberries
crowberries the colour of coal.

I met a boy called *Downy Birch*.

The Colour of Lilac

Look! That's it! That sky smoothing out the sea!
you said (as if we hadn't just watched a man
on his knees apologise to a crowd, and then agree
to polish the cobbles of the street as if they
were walnuts for a daughter's wedding,
to be oiled with attention, with care, and balanced
later in a bowl of blue for the guests,

his face wet with terror, his neck so close
to the stones, to the boots, to the butts of guns
that what I thought of was chalk). I knew
what you were doing, of course but I didn't want
to look. We had been bystanders, watchers,
traitors, silent burners of books, so I let
some window close between us and continued

to walk, listening to the gap between sea and sky
diminish and stretch, diminish and stretch
and diminish. *Don't talk!* I said as you began
again to describe the shade that moved you,
the somewhere between the colour violet
and noonday blues of a sky. *Please!*
Don't talk. So you kept silent as we strode

or as silent as you could with all that cloth
flapping around your ankles. *Absalom*, I wanted
someone to cry (absurd, absurd) *Absalom, Absalom
come on home!* But they didn't, and we didn't,
though we both knew something precious
had been lost that day, something we sought alone
to replenish in the pause between breathing in

and breathing out, as we sat like brothers
awash on the rocks, ignoring the winking town
at our backs and watching the sea-sky darken.
Touching my hand, you said, *We could forgive
each other. We could think of returning home.
We could half close our eyes and pretend this sea
is not the sea, but instead, the lilac of snow.*

how close how far how deep
what shade what shape what height
these quiet skulls like eggs how old
how wide *one hundred thousand*
which angle which side
the walls fall slowly as if half asleep
stepping out of clothes what's heard
what's said *her stained abaya*
from where from when
miles for water what's dug up
who's missing who's quiet
their bed in the crater by the park
what number what cost *on the step a baby*
his sucking mouth what's named what's lost
on the rubbish mound two girls in black
looking for nylon and Pepsi cans
what's counted what's hidden
what's not documented *the boy still searching*
for the head of his dog what's shredded
what's kept which contractor whose job
in the city darkness electric switch click
click whose friend whose father which cellar
which jail *underground the oil* what email
one perfect apricot in the flattened orchard
whose dental record whose record beneath
a new sim card painkillers ninety-nine
prayer beads which faction which cabal
sometimes she tries to get to school
what firm which consortium *at the widow's stall*
petrol by the cup tissues chewing gum
whose ring whose tongue *left by the road*
in his mascara kohl private clothes
what's stolen what's found
a Sumerian statue from the flipflop man
what's ignored *inside there were ants*
what's replayed *the Sony camcorder*
whirring like a watch under her burka

what's intact what's standing what story
what rumour *sepsis making its yellow flower*
which fact which faith *just tea and dates*
tea and dates and three small onions
my son has gone the teacher's leaving
which airport which building
quiet men meeting

Turn

We didn't touch, that night
lying as we were like brides laid out
under our veils, while outside mosquitoes whined
and the long swamps moved and fever trees
swung from the moon. The whites of our eyes
imagined the moon, a frog upturned,
a blown fish, froth breaking out on the waves.

By morning we'd changed. We looked east again
to the sea, our feet clean as the openings of shells.
The water was silver, dunes high and white
the tide smoothing and smoothing the sand.
Wind pulled our hair. We were washed.
We were washed. Dunes struck with light.
Our feet. Lit. Orange. Pink.
The sky filling up with its blue.

Later I watched your footprint fill.
Unmistakeably human, a promise, a turn of the heart,
sole shaped like Africa, the little archipelago
of toes, like mine, like Friday's, as if I were Friday

falling in love, watching the man as he walked,
the heft of him coming down through a foot,
his right, pressing the damp dark sand
so an orbit of light brightened a circle;
then the transfer of weight,
the light going out, while around his left foot,
another circle of sand turning white,
the discarded footprint,
perfect,
lost,

dimming,
filling, losing shape.
Knowing I too left signs.
A necklace of light perhaps.
A scar.

The sun falling fast in the west.
Beasts lifting over the swamp.
No looking back, love.
No looking back.

Ending

Like a hare
big as a deer
there on the hill
in his musculature

Like a hare
in an August field
mown and brown
over a stream
across the gone hill
of a valley

Like a hare
lobbing about
aimless and shorn
among the brown stalks
of a hewn field
over a stream
beyond the gap
of a valley

Stuck out like a thumb
like a deer
on a lawn
a hare in its ears
high on its thigh
drumstick too big
for its body

Jump
jump
like socks on stairs
soft as feet
on faraway floors
dazed like a hare
in the swathe of a field
this way stop

that way look
which way
what way
foot its foot
its long soft foot
its thump its thump
like heart
or boots walking on cloth
or a boat at a pier
that bumps against wood
a hare —

Where?

— beyond the stream
there was a hare
unsure but there
crossing the want
of a valley —

A hare?

— a hare
tall as a deer
and it's disappeared
I don't know where
I don't know where
in the time it took
for you to talk
to say your say
it's gone

Where did it go?
I don't know

Where did it hide?
Perhaps inside
perhaps

in the long-lost hill
of the valley

Possessions

I could have fallen after you down the burrow of your breathing
but something kept shivering beyond my thoughts like a saviour,
a vagrant out of sight, making up stories about the jars and shelving
and forgotten boxes of my life, so it was all I could do to keep
my nerve, eyes glued to the morse of a possible star, and ignore
the moon, blousy and drunk as it was, lurching after clouds
in this strange half-dark, as if a city were approaching
over a hill, or we were that far into summer, that far north
that we mustn't lie still, mustn't rest, any of us, in this leaking
of light from the cracked-open arctic, this melt-coloured sky,
this night half-shut, a sign, like the eye of a man so tired he *must
lie down, must stay awake*, unable to trust we won't steal
his suitcase, any of us that is, except you, so far down in your sleep
the shuffling's nearly stopped on the soft leaf floor of your wood.

News

What are the trees waiting for? This morning
I awoke and the frost had made everything stiff
with its white arthritis, and the sky was still pale
the half-awake sun yet to crank itself over the hill.

And then because of your shock, discovering the news
(which meant I was kind to you, clearing the ice
from your car with a hiss of anti-freeze spray,
cursing myself for not doing the right thing

and using elbow grease and a CD case, let alone
telling you when I first got to know, so it didn't come out
this way, wrong time, when you had somewhere to go)
I missed the sky turning blue, and when I next looked

there were the trees, still as stones but unlike stones, waiting
as if holding breath, as if holding back the release
of an aggression of muscle, bunched tight beneath bark
like sprinters on the block awaiting the crack of a gun

or as if, like a beautiful gang, they'd thrust their intrusions
into the sky blue as ice cream, pleased with themselves
and their bodies, the way only the athletic and beautiful young
can be pleased and cruel with their bodies, and I thought of you

driving all those miles, your heart an old animal clipped by a car,
searching for somewhere small and dark, somewhere to hole up in,
somewhere to lie down, at least until the seaside days
had gone back inside, and the leaping trees had sprung.

Owl Ear

I smile into the dark remembering
how we laughed. And the thought
comes unbidden, like a midnight car park
and a car quietly sliding to a stop
as if to wait, windows up,

that the time will come when one of us
will turn and lay our habit-arm
across the bed in sleep
and find the other is not there.
And in my owl ear the silence,

the absence of your laugh,
its running field, the stream,
the children larking through it,
the plump twins, the skinny runner,
the kid with grazed knee and elbow

triumphant in his tree-top tower,
the tomboy dodging grown-ups
miles behind, to skate across
an empty car park, laughing,
with this to tell her friend –

o happy, hopeless, merry dance

Assassin

Afternoon traffic makes river of the road,
a spool of movement, an unwinding spool
of gingery light. Woman on the bridge looks down
at the water, at dim backs of ducks
marked like shoes. The streetlight floats,
a weather balloon, or an orange
thought. Black water
rocks in its slot. Ducks turn, race
for the light's reflection, breaking it to bits with beaks and feet,
racing away again, copper
leaf,
their own shimmer of photons,
trails, tracks, unravelling
flecks and oils of light.

The woman moves over the bridge,
turns off, following the lane on the hill
for home. Notices the quiet
halfway up,
that she hadn't heard it,
dropping onto the road
at her glittering feet, like a man
who had been walking behind her for days
and was no longer behind her,
but here, in front,
crouched, arms out,
at his back his posse,
his shadow,
his spur-wing geese.

Crocodile

Here I am, watching. Rind of the river, a hardening
scale of water. You mistake me for metal
or wood, a leaf-shaped shallow of gravel.
You don't expect me, here in your city. I wake
from my crater of sleep and wait in the sun,
feeling the redness of rivers run through me.
Crowds rush to look. Loathing slides from tender feet
spreading its oils towards me. I smile. I smile.
I have carried my young in my mouth, my friends.
My nest is secure. My dream-eye closes and opens
in time to the oldest pulse, the shifting
iron of directions. And you over there,
you know it. You know who I am.

You have seen me in the eye of the lizard
my mother, the buzzard my father, the human
in my yellow eye who looks like you, looks so
like you. You could have let go of my gaze
but you knew you were mine, you knew deep down
I would always come and have you dance in the intimate
pallor of underneath-arms, belly to belly, turning
and turning, your head such a gentle weight
against the white of my throat, and I crying
real tears for you, as we sway through the mud
of this inevitable waltz, I closing my eyes
to the yellow-green light as you become me and I become
entirely myself, a rock, a leaf-shaped island of stone.

Disembarking from the 8.09

Whose picture am I in? she asks herself
shouldering her way like a stoat amongst stoats
or a seal amongst seals through the throng
on the platform. She can see the streams
from the towns on the concourse of the station.
She could be a river herself, and go underground.
Open the grille. Slide down right here, feel
the marbelline tiles close over her head, disappear
rat, bat, bug, thin city cockroach spilling
with sistren and brethren down tunnels
of the dark, scuttling and scuttling, joining
and joining, roaring, falling, dividing,
dividing, until the leafy earth is smelt, and sky.

Physician

There is a tinnitus loose
in his house,
a beast that turns and turns,
it lows, it gurns
it moans, it falls
restless, ceaseless, dumb.

Last night he climbed onto its back,
felt twisting saucers of bone,
a floundering neck,
the heave of pelt,
and under his face
wet mane.

He became as soft as a hare,
dreamed through walls of its skull,
lay his long ear
like a leaf on its drum,
and under the roar
deep down deep down,
heard the limp of ambivalent heart.

The animal bore him
round and round,
the animal bore him
round and round,
the animal bore him
round and round and under the sound

half-
heart

half-
heart

half-
heart.

Moving House

It began with the owl moving into the attic
under the chimney where wind lived like an animal,
then the mouse and its offspring bedding down
in softnesses long forgotten in the cellar, then spiders,
many of them, hanging their shadows in string bags
beneath them, touching toes with themselves under lintel
and eave, then flies dead or alive, lining up on the rims
of windows, followed by the flurry of the neighbour
with her autumn Christmas card *The Weeping
Donkey*, then pigeons, whole flocks, and starlings
going nowhere, then the heron elbowing the owl
(now withdrawn deep into the pillow of itself)
along to the furthest reaches of the garret,
then the postman with his post and the ghosts
of the few correspondents and their waiting people,
the community of churches coming in from their places
guarding the status of steeples on the tops of hills,
the yellowing hills, six of them, raggy and dying,
with their listing sheep and other ragamuffins of heather,
the child with her plastic farm, the fuming woman,
the timid woman, the man who doesn't have to say
a word to keep them schtum, the dog and its limp,
the cat, unchallenged king of the cooling car bonnet,
the car beneath its bonnet, tarmac, oil stain, litter, weeds,
wasps stunned by darkness, damp, mould, rot, the loud
and terrible mouths eating and eating, until it became clear
she must pack up her tarpaulin and *trek Ferreira*,
gingerly crossing the stepping stones to a new
rectangle of light, a geometric shape
of empty grass to set up home in,
where, apart from the wind
and the creaking of stars,
it might, for a while,
be quiet.

The Assistant's Confession

When he said *Let it go* I unwound fingers
from the branch like bits of bandage
from a yellow lesion. My wing was broken.
I pinned it carefully to my chest. *Haulage
has its price* he said and stroked my face.

I heard again the sound of deep elastic
stretching beyond any bound, my plastics
snapping. At his question I turned away.
I couldn't tell him I had lost the moon,
how for days I'd hunted under mountains

behind spires and towers and crumbling hills,
how I'd scrabbled through the winter baskets
of every tree, trawled puddles, tunnels, frozen pools.
I also failed to make report of the falling people.
How in the end I turned my back and gazed

at dawn instead – I couldn't bear to do my watch
at the teeming edge, that awful glee, the endless
stream of them, their shirts ballooning,
their little bodies rocking, rocking,
soft as rotten sticks on the rocking jellied sea.

Faith

Unaccountably, things seemed to look up.
He salvaged stone from the ruins and built
three small walls. Where a fourth wall
might have stood he made a sign saying SHOP.

She discovered a smoke-stunned fledgling
under a step. Carrying it was easy
once she knotted a pocket in the hem of her skirt.
Feeding it termites had an immediate effect:
it opened its eyes and she imagined feathers,
birdsong, its own elaborate nest.

As for the other, he pulled himself out of the dust
and made his way down to the river
dragging his leg. There he drank deeply
and washed off the ash, combing his hair backward
with careful hands. He buttoned his shirt
right up to the neck, and fashioned a crutch
from a blackened branch. He returned to the shop,
and bowed to the others, joining their circle,
singing their songs of love and redemption
even as new flames topped the horizon.

Benjamin's Pool

Coming back from the land
he looked up at the violet hills
at the resounding sky above the hills
and the light said (or was it the way

he perceived the light, suggesting
a meaning that sounded itself
like a voice in his head, a quiet,
known, forgotten voice, a voice

naming physics of city
and wilderness, silence and rivers,
and rivers flowing to the absolute
reliability of returning sea,

the return of rain and stone
also therein) *Stop Benjamin, rest*
for a second, and see me, see me,
let me in! This was not God

speaking. He knew this from the way
the falling slate of his brain
sliced open a bubble of laughter,
and he winked at himself

with the steady blue eye of himself,
suddenly in love with the wryness
of his own skew, shrug face.
But he did rest, nonetheless

he chose to rest against the wall
and watch the light of hills, that sky
falling like slow sand over the dark
blue fold of the hills, looking

with all of himself, seeing
with feet, throat, chest, lips, skin,
gazing as if he was drinking
water from a small pool found

amongst rocks, amongst dust
and rocks at the centre of continents,
a pool where he might have lain
in thirst and seen his face

seen the hills and sky behind his face,
where he might at last have drunk
through and from behind his face,
as if he'd never drink in light again.

II

Acres

Acres

I

Who's side are you on, Mrs Mimosa? You failed to explain
that her feet would weep in the languor of hay-fever moons.
I have watched her tire, the horse of her droop, listless, breathless,
hauling her terror and disgust for so long over disinterested hills.
She has stretched as far as she can with her newly gloved hands,
but they are deceptive, septic, will shame us tomorrow
when the real work starts and the athletes converge for the showdown.

You misled us with calm, Mrs Mimosa, as if failure follows like day
follows night, inevitable, neutral as breathing. Why didn't you warn
of the bloat, the twist of a body that has used the last of its lightning?
Or the thing that happens to limbs when the dribble of will dries up,
the smell of flesh, the yesterday smell of parlours. She weakens,
Mrs Mimosa, a leylandii-black in her brain keeps her awake,
an oozing under her skin, she is becoming a snail, she is punctured.

And you with your tranquil hair, shifting your silks so the light
fills the creases and flows to your feet like water. Please! Don't return
to sketching the hills! I do what I can! I whistle as sweetly as ever
in the yellow-pink sea of the field, I take off my shirt, I bend
and lift hay, I catch angles of light on my body. I have always
made sure my muscles slip over my muscles as I wade knee-deep
in the sward, and I sweat, I sweat, just like the man in her picture.

Yes, we all hear the grinding of change: the gulf stream reverses
direction. But you saw her this morning when I swore I'd beaten
her dwindling bounds. The acres we salvaged together! She's not
blind.
She listens for the march of the athletes. She watches the tremors
travelling the grass, feels the shift of the hills through her bedstead.
The athletes are coming, Mrs Mimosa. Rings shiver the water,
sky turns the colour of helmets. Rouse her! Help me, Mrs Mimosa!

II

Cheerful and queenly
I will be there,
dressed in fuchsia
for the future of families.
I will sit in the wide chair
lit by the lilac window,
arms replete, resting
lightly as loaves
over the folds of peacock brocades,
while the long hounds
remain solicitous and watchful beside me,
solicitous and watchful,
their sly heads moving
offset by the debut of collars.
God console me I will cry,
laughing at the stamping thighs
of my athlete, admiring from afar
the powerful brushwork of her brows
God console me Child,
surely it's never as bad as all that!

And when the shadows move
with balaclavas into the room,
when the French doors
turn crimson, ivory, leaden,
when every echo is muffled
by the deafening snow, and owls
like moths slide past my face
and down the darkening window,
I will call through the glass – *Child!*
through rooms and acres – *Child!*
God console me Child I will call,
Where are you?
Where are you?
Where did you go?

Cut it well back, Garsonne, back to the root.
There's nothing more galling than hedges
half-pruned. And Child, out of my sightline!
Can you not see the hills piling the horizon
like heaps of new fish? They are there to glisten,
to be viewed – a vista, a picture, a prospect
not to be missed! Oh run along, run along.
And for pity's sake stop opening and closing
those toes. Garsonne, does she not know
how to wear shoes? Can she not simulate grace?
She's practically feral. Look at her now,
her stiff hands, her tight face. No, she won't do

in the house. It's a waste but you'll have to
take over from Mrs Mimosa and train her outside.
Perhaps she could herd the cattle, the sheep?
Perhaps she could husband the geese?
God knows it's a pity, those plummeting eyes.
She didn't come cheap. I'll miss the sound
of her breath, the charm of arms flung back
when she sleeps. But awake at close quarters
Garsonne, it cannot be borne. Those muscular
frowns, those furious shins! You should hear
the rasp of her teeth when she moans, the roll
of her tongue when I insist she refrain from her song.

How she glints, how she glints! I've had moments
Garsonne. Am I mad, are we safe in our beds?
It's those underground eyes, that predatory
tilt of the head. If she were a man –
Mrs Mimosa will tell you how she holds a bone
in her hands! I shudder to think, I shudder
to think, Garsonne. No. I'll watch from afar
from the orange room. She will look splendid
under the sun. But she must come to no harm.
Teach her to harvest, to water, to dig. Check
fences. The hedge. And I will think about dogs
Garsonne. Yes. A pair of appropriate dogs.

Arguing with Malarchy

Prologue

Mackenzie moved like a sleuth with the bird through Milan
avoiding the station. Taxi to Padua, and Verona
reached by late-night bus. Mud-flats barefoot

were a tortuous business. Like following dark arms
of a half-drugged dancer in an ill-lit opera
or riding the back of an eel. Like rot.

Like slipping down branches of an unknown version
of the tree of life, damp as the skin of a fever,
or hugging the walls of a tunnel off the shaft

of a mine that no longer yields tin
but according to myth conceals gold. After
three days, he made it to Venice. Here he stayed put.

Taking the bird from his pocket he fed it with corn.
Saw clouds in its eyes. After the heist it hadn't recovered
the sheen on its plumage, now it was the colour of dust.

He tried cream of artichoke heart, tongue-fish and warm
panettone. He took it at night to the golden basilica,
and prayed incognito to saints. Hired a blind violinist

to play *Lark Ascending* and 'Spring' from *Four Seasons*
and when the little bird died, rented a gondola
for a moonlit funeral. With casket clasped to his chest

Mackenzie wept for all that was lost, singing hymns
in English whatever the danger. Rocking over milk-black water
the thin boat slid. Still weeping, he asked to get out.

Careless of bearings he wandered labyrinthine
streets. Heard water sucking on steps. Didn't run for cover
when a loudspeaker said: *Mackenzie, you're under arrest!*

Old Man Advises Malarchy on the Contents of the Will

Overtime overtime
debit and credit
production
consumption – wait –
Gordon Bennett!
Enclosed in the cabinet
what do we find?
Postcards, list, a whiff of spirit,
the makings of my testament!

Who do I love, who do I love
how much can I measure in decimal pounds
in hands, in ells, in ounces?
There are only five, Malarchy
only five, and it's tricky my boy
to divide the world in the head.

Spain ahoy, or is it Cape Verde
peninsula, island, promontory, spit
headland, outcrop
tongue, neck, point?
Easy, sailor, take it slow
the waves collapse on an unreliable shore
the sands are sucked by a toothless moon
and marsh reeds bend to the left of the sound
a skeletal tune in a skeletal wind
so gently sailor, take it slow. Are you sure
are you sure you know?

It's Mackenzie, Malarchy, crossing the road.
He's carrying a cage without any bird
but the wisp of a song
wafts like a feather of smoke
from between the bars. Is it hers, Malarchy?
Is it hers? Those trembling notes
the colour of heather, the colour of water
the colour of cloud, move through the song
of an absent bird, over the eyes of the remembered lover

the forgotten girl, the knuckling dead
the drunken drinkers wanting bread
the eaters that eat the hate uneaten
by the ghost the god the goat.
Oh Malarchy! Get that goat!
Drain the blood in the proper way.
Another bird was lost today.

One two
three four five
two for the sand dune
two for the wave
and one for my esteemed Malarchy
with this advice: Avoid Mackenzie!
Keep belief, my darling boy
and tell the soldier and the sailor
there's no more money in the meter.
Now lift the feather
from the dusty floor
and place it over my mouth.

Old Man Describes to Malarchy his Coming of Age

I came of age, Malarchy, when I gave up my borrowed clothes,
took off the red coat my mother had sewn for me, my father's
unsuitable shoes. I went anonymous, awol, deserted, following
a fool till I saw him slip underground. How had I known?

Picked up in clubs, in my youth, I had been shown messages
in sawdust, written with desultory feet. Scuffed over easily
in improvised fights or drunken dancing, these told of doors
in the wall, the floor, the lids, the hidden trapdoors, the signs

you must give. For a fuck in the dark, I received instruction
on making the break, on the spur, double quick. Avoiding
the army, stadia, police, the taxman, the drugs man, the bailiffs,
the hoods, tagging, grassing, orange suits, radars, cameras

heat-tracking beasts. The ways to distinguish between them
and us, to see the future, to deny the past. How to get to the coast,
how to hijack a lorry. Leave in the lurch. Invent a story. Lie low
in a madhouse, survive at the Pole. The most discreet ways

to follow a fool. So here I am, Malarchy, wet from the bath,
being wrapped in the steam you hold in your arms, whispering
how it was I found you, blind, staggering drunk, patched hat
and balloon zigzagging towards the manhole I followed you down.

Old Man Argues with Malarchy about Certainty

It's all very well, Malarchy, telling me to feel the weight,
the shape, the satisfying certainty of the small smooth stone
in my hand. It's a very commendable thing, pointing out
as you do, the absence of skin, or scale, or fur on a stone

which means it's itself, it's itself, all the way through to its stone.
But what about the patriot's law, Malarchy? And what
of soldiers, scholars and their scrolls, the half-hidden
swords that emerge in pixel dots on X-ray machines? What

does your stone reveal about these, Malarchy? What?
Can't you hear the far-off roaring of prayer in churches
synagogues, mosques, the muffled sound of bodies clubbed
by anonymous cars, the hoods, the silence like churches

when delete keys press on names of enemies of church
or state? And what of the people who have no doubt
even with the smooth black shell of the timer, safety catch
off, its numbers red, segmented and square, marking (no doubt

like clockwork) the death of seconds under their arms? Doubt
not the terror or love of their mothers, minds stunned by countdown
to terrible zero, relentless, relentless, the losing, their child. You're
                                                                              hurt
Malarchy. I'm sorry. But your stone doesn't speak to me. I'm down

on my luck with your stone. It is dumb to me. Dumb. I'm putting
                                                                         it down.

Old Man Informs Malarchy of the Effects of Sound

It will all come out in the wash.
I only heard half, Malarchy, but her subject
was confusion of fish. Cacophonies
under the seas she said, have knotted up song,
webs are tearing, turtles go wandering,
the sirens of submarines leave rings
of confusion and radars of sharks go wrong.
Cupped in a satellite dish, undersea operas
are miming, whales swim alone, swim dumb,
swim dumb, the clubs of themselves thud the shore.

And on land there's a bird, Malarchy —
is she there any more? I can hardly remember
the notes that spilled like sweets on the half-furled
tongue of my ear. I can't hear her
Malarchy, I can't hear. Is she clasped in the horn
of Mackenzie's hand? Does she sing for him
or make no sound or then again is everything drowned
in the din? An ear of an elephant is concealed
in its feet, that is a fact, Malarchy,
we should take note, we should take note.

Old Man Complains to Malarchy about Maths

Things don't always transform, Malarchy!
It isn't art! It's just incorrect. Inaccurate.
You have to respect figures and facts —
you cannot subtract the number five
from the number five and expect
an answer of *point one point two*. You may
like the sound, but there are absolute factors
to take into account, for instance,
there is only one place for a decimal point,
numbers aren't words we can bend like reeds
to our will. Five from five is nought, Malarchy —
nil, nix, zilch, nowt, love, void, zero,
absence, absence, nothing at all…

Old Man Instructs Malarchy on How to Pray

No I'm not panicking. But tell him it's up
to our waists. While we're lucky its summer
its never summer for ever, not even out here
and where does he think we are, the Atacama
the Sahara, the Thar? I can hear it lap
in my sleep, as if your ribcage is a tottering pier

or the peeling keel of a dinghy awaiting a sail,
and tell him I am watching the water darken
your shirt an inch above its reflection. Where's
too far, Malarchy? Ask him! Tell him of the rota
to keep singing and awake; how your idea
of imitating calls of lapwings, gulls, marsh harriers

is getting us precisely nowhere. They're not pigeons,
not doves, and we are no saints of Assisi.
Chimneys diminish. I'm watching trees disappear,
a wind-up gramophone float by, in pieces,
a shape like a caravan tipped on its back in the region
of the Mount. Tell him, Malarchy, how I fear

the meaning of these things, and if we're not found, well
just say this: you may be blind, and I believe nothing
but the worst, but we both notice your prayer
remains unanswered. The sun is drowning
again and still no bargain struck. Sky full
as a bell, but empty. My legs swell, veneer

peeling off. And you there rooted, arms afloat
like upturned fish, holding the moon in your eyes
while water milks your beard. Oh no. Not tears.
Not now, Malarchy! Chin up, chin up! We'll find a sign.
Nothing so fancy as lilo or log, or heaven forbid a boat
that floats. But something. Keep talking. He'll hear.

Old Man Muses to Malarchy on a Sleepless Night

Is it the way the clouds elapse
or the elision of wind and rain?

With liminal fingers I can draw a map
of your back, but never, I know, draw mine.

Do you hear the owl in the valley tonight
the tube of its call reaching far

to the winds of the bleak North Sea. Who
does it allude to, Malarchy, could it be you?

Or is it the dancer who elopes
with intruders, the fabulous sailor

who breaches the borders of the moon's white
road on the waves? I see a boy in the hood

the hood, dementing in the cloths
of its dark. There is cork in this wine, Malarchy

and the drugs for the pain do not work.
I need sleep, I need sleep. To dream again

of that which matters, the woman
with skirts like the rings of Venus

who spun in men's arms like a kingfisher
spins when diving for fish in the stream.

Or the orbit of bird, first black and then white
as it turns inside out and light

falls on the slope of its turning wing.
I went wrong, Malarchy. Oh I went wrong.

Old Man Speaks to Malarchy of Defeat

Listen, Malarchy – they were out to get me!
Mackenzie in his prime, slapping his horse,
his cohorts in crimson, greasing their saddles,
greased boots reflecting the red-mouthed guffaws
of men on a border. I hadn't a chance.
Peeled and unbuttoned they swung me
above them, lanced like a pig on the bone of a tree.
I finally landed, compliant as liver, saw horse muscle
wince. Held the white of its eye for minutes.
Coming to from my dreams there is bound to be flailing.
Please leave me alone. There's the split of the moon.
Leave the sheet. The bed sheet, Malarchy!
And the last of the whisky. Yes – of course he won.

Old Man Reveals to Malarchy the Art of Flying

I take my mind into the mountains, Malarchy,
where weather should dissolve into stone
and stone disappear into weather. But what I remember
are sparks on the water, the gulp and lap
as I lie on my plank looking up at the rock,
the etch of itself so clear on blue, that I can see
lichen, moss in a crevice, cracks on the surface,
outlines of peaks and summits like buildings
of a city unfinished, roofs I could reach
if I ran at the boulders like stairs, the ledge
where I'd crouch as a buzzard might perch,
feeling the edge, the urge to open, to spread,
to unpack from the scapula impulse and feather
and compressions of leather and sail, and lift

lift, the heft of wind bearing the load
of arms made wide, and of course it isn't
Mackenzie who comes to mind, Malarchy,
but Icarus, Icarus, run to the mountains,
feeling their angles like wings within him,
the thinning air planing his bones, inflating

his chest, finding the magnet he thought he'd lost,
his measuring eye, his subtle wrist,
his fingers' gap, his spinnaker shirt,
and from the corner of his eye
he thinks he sees a plummeting ghost,
or is it his God coming to rest
in the quiet white of the sun?
He jumps, Malarchy. Yes. He jumps.

Old Man Disagrees with Malarchy about Age

Half full? Half full? Don't be a fool, Malarchy,
this isn't a question of attitude!
The process involved is biological –
nothing magical can be done to stop it,
no prayer, no charm, no amulet, tablet,
and perception it definitely isn't!
Love changes nothing, Malarchy.
It's tick, it's tock! These are the facts. Clock:

lesions occur in the DNA, cells repair in a slipshod way,
gums recede, arteries harden, joints inflame, ligaments shorten,
infarct, stroke, tumour, falls, cataracts, floods,
sphincters fail, vagueness, madness, terror,
death. Vagueness, madness –

Don't dance, Malarchy, please,
please, don't dance.
You waste my breath
with your la la la-ing
your spin spin spinning
your flip flip flipping
your fou fou fouing
your ha- ha- ha-ing
your singing
your singing –
for pity's sake, *peace!*

I'm not crying.

Yes, your sound does move
the water
and the dim fish
do quiver

– yes.

Do you feel the fish,
the water, with your fingers?
Your blind face
trembles when you sing, Malarchy,
your blind, lit, wet face.
Peace boy,
peace,
peace.

Old Man Asks Malarchy about Truth

Even as I say it I doubt the veracity –
I can no longer remember the sequence, Malarchy
or whether flickering events happened at all.
Instead I watch shadows of animals
migrate over the wastes of my bedroom wall
and trudge the deserts searching in vain
for the flash of a wing of a skirt
of a song the wheel of a bird
or a lost balloon drifting like thought past my head.

Extinct, Malarchy, is all of it dead?
And what of the sailor searching the sand
on skeletal dunes of a shipwrecked land
what of the click of threadclaw feet
the orange tap of orange beak
the glassy burn of brilliant eye
viridian sheen of feather?
And the heather, the heather
her song, Malarchy
falling softly like rain…

What of the waters
up to the neck
the hood the hood
the horse's flesh
what of the fish
the numbers lost
the washed-up
splay of Icarus?

The hat. The hat.

The keeping faith.

Milk of mouth.

Smoke of breath.

What of the light of fall on cloth
drape
drop
shadow
at all is there something in what I recall
overtime overtime
postcard list
fragment backroom
splinter bit talk
riven the remnant
patches
patches of mind –

Is that Mackenzie, Malarchy?

Mackenzie?

Malarchy?

Malarchy?

The Desert Chronicles

I

What she didn't say was where she went,
the dog she took (the jackal-cross), her mount
part wildebeest, part Appaloosa horse.
The thought she put into trek supplies
(knife, hat, billycan, maps of watercourses,
of southern stars). What she didn't say

was how she followed airborne geese,
the spoor of bushpig, dik-dik, oribi,
and on cloudy days the call of hadedas,
or flight paths of undecided moths.
And once a stately swarm of bees
took her over veld to the forest edge

where she came upon a man in camouflage,
asleep, a soldier on the run who stole
her saddlebag, and would have snatched
the horse as well, if the jackal had not barked
and given chase; which brought her
thoughts back sharply to the camp

(she had been absorbed in a line of ants
transporting crumbs of samp and meat
from her tin plate to a red hole in the ground).
They travelled onward, mapless now,
skirting see-through hives of city lights
and if they stumbled on a rural settlement

leopard-crawling round it, or holing up
till dark. Bushes thinned. Grass grew sparse.
Ennui began to settle a haze of khaki dust
until a jewel-beetle winked at them, wings
glinting in the dirt. Enchanted,
they zigzagged after it, following its path.

Then the beetle disappeared. They blundered
to a stop. For the first time for hours
they looked up. Sand. Sand. Dune
upon dune in uneasy wind, under sun
like a white-hot spoon, air unsteady, dangling
unsteady ground. They were lost. Nothing

found to follow but staring sun by day,
by night the staring moon. Once they saw
a desert rat but the jackal snapped its neck
with a single crack of jaws and before
the moisture could be licked, it was sucked out
by the sand. Then the horse went down.

II

What she didn't expect was relief
bubbling up like a spring discovered
under a rock in this darkening desert,

the calm sweeping in
like a brush of rain, this knowing
there was nothing more to be done,

except to remove the horse's bridle,
to stroke his face, to cradle his head
and sing with the jackal as it sang

pulling the moon over the dunes
with its savannah song. She would hold
the horse's gaze, give her attention

to keeping pain at bay.
And when the horse was ready
to close his eyes she too would rest,

and count, and contemplate the broken
stars until the stars began to hurt.
Then she'd lie down on her side

under the horse's flickering heart,
so from above she'd be a scan
of unborn colt, the jackal

curling in her arms, a diagram
in chalk, her unborn child,
and like this they'd each attend

to the progress of sun and moon,
to shadow, light, to heat and cold
and bit by bit their minds would close

leaving sand and wind to blow
to clean their bones and shift the dunes
and slowly change the lines of land

until they were a clasp of shell
uncovered on the shore.
The sea would come.

Nothing more now to be done.
Nothing more now
to be done.

III

That isn't how it went. She came to.
And watched horizons pass her by
as if she dozed on a childhood raft,
drifting down some old canal or lazy river
winding round its yellow hill. Felt the lift

and fall of jackal ribs, all fur and leather
beneath her arm, the panting Appaloosa pelt
scraping at her salted spine. All alive! All
on the move, a finger's width above the sand
as if transported on a swatch of air, a pall

or sleeping mat she couldn't see, rocking
gently, gently rocking. No. Impossibility.
She closed her eyes and thought of home,
all the words she might have said. But still
they moved. She raised her head. Gone –

the sand dunes gone. Instead, a drifting skyline
of piled-up stone, a small ravine, mauve
and pink against the sky, sickle-thorn
and bitterbush, and was that mutter water,
this, mud on the creeping ground?

The wildebeest thrashed to its knees,
the jackal-cross twisted and stood. All three
crawled to the waterfall, lay facedown and drank.
Then they turned to greet their saviour.
What they found were soldier ants.

The colony turned and streamed away,
like the world's first serpent, stately, slow.
Or a wide black river winding round some yellow hill.
And the horse, the dog, the woman turned back
to the waterfall, bathed, gazed, and drank their fill.

IV

Back home, the shadows of the beech leaves fell like pools
upon the lawn, the evening sun's warm linen lying soft
across her arm. At his desk through the bay window
he continued noting down his thoughts on genes
and female hormones, neural pathways, lithium.

A cuckoo called. Swallows drew tomorrow-maps
with ink-dipped, skyward wings. She watched the trance
of tiny flies as they swung above the pond. Now and then
she felt him glance at her, as if he hoped to catch her eye,
but she found she preferred to sink into the luscious

fumbling of the bees. There he was again, blocking
out her view. *I've brought you jasmine tea my dear.*
May I sit down? She smiled vaguely, stood, and hurried down
the slope, following the fat dachshund that had been sleeping
at her feet. She heard him shout her name behind her,

but the tongues of sun upon the lawn
were lapping the long shadows, and calling her to come.
And she was nearly at the paddock where her old Welsh pony
grazed. The dachshund barked. The pony raised its head,
whinnied, and met them champing at the gate.

The Naming of Ages

I knew before I began
this would be seen
as the age of chickens.
We have had times
you and I, not named
for birds: aeons of wells
walls, mountains, cities.
Sometimes we have tried
to wrest an age
from its proper name,
unhinged by stubbornness
or a seam of longing.
But perhaps there's little
in the end to be done:
perhaps an age is an age
named for itself, whatever
our effort or intention.
But imagine (what if)
imagine this had been
the age of starlings.
Herons. Guillemots.
What would we have done?
What else, my darling,
might we have found?

debut

small feather
long stalk
warm leaf
whole
sleek
come trouble
come coffin
come old woe

nothing today
closes its lid
or dulls the sun
the dandelion

sky wide
settles down
over hills blue as easter
cotyledons
stand on tiptoe
(tiptoe)
trees pricked
ready to go

and we all wait for the chicks to cross the threshold

here they come
stepping out of the house
highstepping over
the colour green
yellow and ginger and
proud
of their huge
new
shoes

Travelling with Chickens (I)

Coming back this time it's more difficult
not to get lost, as if there is leakage.

Night after night I wake up, heart jumping
and wait for the scops owl calling the time

the bushbaby's weeping. Last night I dreamt
I sat under a baobab, my back to its hide

as if I was leaning against my friend
the elephant, both of us dozing in the heat of the day

with you little hen, pecking at our feet
and Delores and HP and the rest of the chickens

scratching away under the nearby yellow mopani.
And for all the world we looked as if

this was where we each belonged, so when in the distance
we heard a fish eagle keening its sorrow

it was right you stood still, and looked up, wings braced
for take-off as if you'd been called, and I saw

the afternoon blue of the sky moving over your eyes
until you remembered, and turned to me

who you found had also remembered;
how you bent your head as if you were praying for me

or us, or the others, or perhaps for the fish eagle
killing again, the flicking wet length of its prey.

Waiting for Cure

I am waiting for the remedy to work
in the cockerel whose breathing is drowning.

I remember that evening when light slewed
across the flatness of marshes

like trajectories of javelins thrown low and long,
the warnings of people beyond the horizon.

How the conversation moved between the three of us,
of a heart repeatedly broken, habits of lifetimes,

amygdalas shrunken like fruits of uprooted trees.
Salt. Holes. Water stolen. Stolen shade. How we passed

under an old brick bridge that spanned the canal,
Ann was crying, and evening laid its net on the water.

The reflections on the red brick shook, and looking up
I saw a swarm of bees at work, ghosts of bees,

wings giant, close up, as if we were in the heart of the hive
and so for a moment I forgot about everything else,

the brick was aquiver with the loudness of light,
it was form with the sound turned down;

no substance but movement, depth but no weight,
this swarm an illusion of sadness maybe, a confusion

of fury and light. You said my name, I took your arm
and Ann took mine. Now I hold the bird close,

and wait. There's a mire in his lungs.
All creatures need more than one chance.

Travelling with Chickens (II)

It's cold, February clutched around the land.
The hen's feathers click like styrofoam,
her feet, small reptiles, balance on my hand.
She eyes me with a tunnel eye. I gauge the opening
at its end. Down we go. Through rings of brown
and gold, I walk out to October, the canal, its yellow
veil of leaves, a man in a canoe waving me to come,
holding his thin boat steady. I step in. A crow
lands, shuffles on my shoulder. We slide on. Sky
sun, leaves, trees split open, let us pass
and knit again behind us, shivering. On the towpath
a narrow-bodied dog runs on shadow, keeping time.
I touch the crow. Ahead of us the black and hole
of tunnel. We enter. Hen and I emerge. February. Cold.

Extending the Pond

You dig a hole to extend the pond
as if in search of something
that someone loving buried long ago
underneath the beech
on our allotment.

And the sun comes out
(as it often seems to do just before it drops
behind the hills) and where it falls
between the leaves, it reddens all
the browns and yellows
in your hair, and I watch
the smallest hen sink
upon the slow hydraulics of her legs
so her cushion comes to rest
on the breadth of your resting shoulder,
while the other birds continue scuffing
round your feet murmuring
in what seems to be companionship,
and what I want to do
is to join you all in the ongoing task
but am afraid I'll shake the surface
of the evening's trust,
and so I wait a little and watch your progress
as the sun goes down,
till you turn, and see me,
smile, and wave to me to come.

the radio says tonight it will rain
already the water's in spate

the way it runs off the field
      and under the road
          into the trough
              onto the furrow made from a gutter
                and into the dug-out pool

could be described as   *full*
                     fulfilled
the space occupied   *fulfilled*
by water
fat
with water

the last light filling it
    the moving sky behind the light
        blue with it
            the water a see-through tube of tree and sky and light
and blackbird flying between and for that one moment huge
in it

the water filled
        full
        full with everything else
but itself
    itself